Ephemeral Village

by Daniel Ausema

October 25, 2024

Island of Wak-Wak

Island of Wak-Wak
Örebro, Sweden
www.islandofwakwak.com

October 2024

Cover Art: *Mainz — Winter Scene*, 1892
by Charles Leikert (1816–1907)

Typeset using KOMA-Script & LaTeX 2ε.
Printed via Books on Demand.
www.bod.se

ISBN: 978-91-989598-4-0

Tryck: Libri Plureos GmbH, Hamburg,
Tyskland

Contents

Dedication

These poems are dedicated to all those whose sense of identify and home wanders in and out of the mist.

Ephemeral Village

The Village of the Mists

Our ancestors built our homes
on a human-made hill,
a terp of scrap lumber and fill dirt,
generations of trash lifting us
above the brackish flooding.
To float a span above the ground.

What arcane power did they anger?
Or what magic did they capture
in the layers of dirt and debris?

For our homes refuse to rest.
The terp wanders like a fishing boat
with a broken moorline.
Never part of the world, we meander
from fog to mist at uncanny angles
set off from reality.

Unsettled settlement.

The False Island

It only appears by foglight,
at first like an island in the mist
where no ship ever runs aground,
defying our memories and history
hadn't we . . . how could it . . .

It comes closer, fog after fog,
disappearing in daylight,
invisible under the moon,
but creeping toward us
each time the fog returns.
And fog always returns here;
we wear it on our skin,
breathe mist for air, pump
its vapors through our veins.

Like the false island,
fog is expert at betraying history
and mocking memory.
Of the three — memory, fog, and history —
fog has always been
the only reliable one.

Widdershins

Those who climb the false hill on the wrong side,
attempting to escape the uncanny
ambiguities and impossibilities of the island
by sneaking in through the lee of the fog and up,
find only façades.

Shopkeepers sell them nothing.
The clock on the tower runs backward.
The bells toll without sound.
Linger, and a herd of silent cows
will follow the interloper
wherever they go,
gathering more cattle the longer it takes.
Eventually
the blank stares of the growing herd
forces them to flee.

Only by accepting the uncertainties
of mist and mystery at the village gate
can a visitor climb to find the true village.

As much as any of it is real.

For the Villagers, from Afar

He falls in love with the washer woman,
hanging pristine clothes in the mist,
her face so still and peaceful as she works;
he does not know that washing is
merely a fraction of her busy life
of social visits and keeping the books
for her brother's laundry business,
that her keen eyes have earned far more
than her clothes hanging—
but that she is valued for both.

He falls in love with the woodcutter,
the man's hands steady and strong,
beneath the stacks of firewood;
he does not know that the lines of logs,
meticulous and orderly, are his escape
from the chaos of caring for children—
his own and those of two other families—
a breath of outside air before he returns,
again present and alert for his charges.

He is in love with the village at a distance,
in love with the surfaces of the outside lives
of the villagers on the uncanny terp
as it wanders across the fields he knows so well.
He doesn't dare approach the village,
knowing it will shatter his constructed loves.

The War of Fog and Sea

Why does the sea wish to conquer the fog?
To turn its swirls into salt,
to venture over the land and find
the renegade waves that hide in dry spaces.

Why does the fog wish to pull the sea from its bed?
To blanket the land in obscurity,
to sow fields of salt and to harvest
nothing ever more.

In the Streets of Mist

If you are allowed to climb
into the ephemeral village,
give your legs time to adjust
to the movement of soil and paving.

Do not dismiss your dizziness
as merely an effect of the mist.
The village moves,
though you cannot see it,
cannot see the hidden land
as you pass through, wandering
over sea and back to shore.

But even time
will not let you truly settle into steadiness.
As long as you remain,
you'll feel the strange sense
of being a stranger,
of visiting a place not meant
for you or me.

The Tricksters of Ice and Fog

The locals may caution you,
Beware the edges of the village,
the ground unstable, the air currents wild.

What they neglect to warn visitors of
is the beings that live in the fog,
essences of ice and malice,
stirring up the winds to make them
deadly.
It is not the currents themselves to blame,
but the fog ones driving the air wild.

What they neglect to prepare visitors for
is the tricksters that hide away in their homes,
foundation folk that come from their nests
to frighten strangers.
They mean no harm, but enjoy
the wobbly way of unsteady ground,
the shock of a falling visitor, pushed from the edge.

Why do they leave these things out?
It may be that the villagers, too, have a touch
of trickster blood in their veins, and a frenzy
of icy fog, pent up in their lungs.

Old News

The village crier is the last to hear news,
the one who misses every rumor,
who remains blissfully unaware
until everyone else knows each detail.

Then he announces the old news
for all to know.

The villagers joke that he only proclaims
a new marriage after the divorce
has been filed.
But do not take it for mockery.
They speak with affection and hear his words,
for it is only when he announces news
that they know
how to modulate their gossip,
how loud to whisper
the news of today, the news of tomorrow.

The Sweet Falsities

Do not ask
the old ones who tend the ovens
for a taste of pastry.

Do not ask the silent one,
stirring the dough into the oil,
what the ingredients are
or where they are sourced.

The scent of raisins is enough,
the smell of cooling dough and almonds,
the sprinkle of sugar to top it off.

Do not ask the name of the smiling baker
standing woodenly behind the counter,
only taste the deep-fried fog,
the finger-scorching pastries
made of clouds and memory,
the sweet falsities of our ephemeral village.

The Wordless Words of Protection

A predator has appeared
in the adjacent lands.
It hides beneath the village,
darting out for prey as the ephemeral ground
moves over the land.
No one knows exactly what it is.
Feline? Ferret? Fae?
It is skittish and swift
and flees the sound of a human voice.

The prey in adjacent lands
have learned to imitate
the wordless chatter
of shopkeepers cleaning,
of villagers calling a greeting,
of passersby from a distance.

Many in the village have begun to hear voices
and wake to memories
of loved ones long dead.

Truths From Dreamland (an onzijn)

By foglight comes the village across the strand
dispersing night fowls, scattering the field mice,
and bending dry reeds aside so it can pass.
Those who enter find wonders but no device,
no arcane wizardry, magic looking glass,
or nightly chant to explain its wanderings.
Those who seek no certainty in the bent grass
and fog swirls find instead their own answerings,
transitory and wordless truths from dreamland.
The village poses nomadic riddles, runes
of uncanny fog, dark moors, and haunting loons.

The Memory of Folk Art

The folk art of the surrounding towns
features flowers painted on painted plates,
colorful whimsies to brighten the day's chores.
Where the village has passed through,
a shadow blurs the delicate flowers,
petals grow unnatural shapes,
strange creatures peek out from behind
the discolored stems.
The village moves away, and the townsfolk
forget its unsettling presence,
only remembered in the uncanny details
of their art of decorative plates.

The Baker's Story

A pastry for you, another for him,
and if the oven is cooling, and if
the rush of the morning has eased,
and if the coffee is the almost black
of the fog bank two hours after sunset,
then he'll sit and tell his story.

It is a story of leaving and returning,
of the lure of mists, the hook of home,
of sweet doughs and crushed almonds,
and the heat of the oven cutting through the cold.

But it is not a tale of words alone,
not one that can be transcribed in poetry,
for he kneads the words with silences,
lets the fragments rise and crush, proof and bake.
The pauses and grunts and wordless assents
are a part of the secret recipe of his story.

Thoughtless

Let your thoughts be like the fog—
  dense and formless,
  damp with unknowledge.
Let your thoughts be like the village—
  wandering without a goal,
  filled with odd life and mystery.

An Ephemeral Triptych

The right panel

shows only fog,
the swirls of gray vary
into fractals of chaos,
hinting only at deeper
layers of more fog,
no hidden meaning,
no truths rising from the depths.

The central panel

displays the village itself,
brown silhouettes wrapped in mist
with steep roofs of tile and thatch;
a hint of a dirt road peeks
from the bottom of the panel,
a wheelbarrow leans against a wall,
a clothesline disappears into the fog
as if it has no endpoint, the green
of amorphous vegetation drips with damp.

The left panel

writhes against the other two,
an un-panel of formlessness
growing and shrinking as it tries
to envelop the full painting;
it is what the right panel wants to be,
incorporeal swirls of vapor;
is what the central panel fears,
the uncontrolled chaos
of subatomic interactions
made visible, entropy encroaching.

The Island's Leading Edge

Braggarts in nearby villages
claim to climb the constructed hill
as the village heads to sea.

The hunting is supreme, they say,
whale and seal and colossal sturgeon.

Or it's the only way to see
the sea's mermaids, combing their hair
in the spray that comes off the island.

Or the villagers do it for the thrill,
the crash of waves, the way the ground
becomes something else — a transition
between corporeal and intangible —
beneath their feet, giving them a glimpse
beyond.

None of the boasters have ever done
what they claim. But it's possible
that some villagers have.
Look
for the haunted cast to their faces,
the way their eyes shy away from yours,
the phasing in and out of their fingers
as they fidget beneath your gaze.

The Myth of Sunlight

Some say the sun,
warm and pleasant,
will burn away the fog
that shrouds the island
someday; that the village
will join the solid world
of fields and dikes and
towering windmills.

Those who know more of
the ways of fog and fen
know that the sun is a myth,
that its light is merely
another kind of fog,
distant and fleeting and false.

Harvest While You May

Gather in the fog in a basket,
harvest the wisps of mist,
take up the vapors in careful pleats,
and hold them before you, suddenly shy.

Take from the clouds as they sweep down
the button berries of hailstones,
the loaves of cumulus fog,
and eat while there is anything to taste.

Family Histories

Those who live on the moving hill
trace their descent from a fairy king
and the mortal he tricked into marriage.

They live in that memory, of shame
and betrayal, and magical might.

Or from a crane pair transformed
into human semblance, so that
their lives are spent longing

for open skies above the fog,
for feathered nests and long flights.

Or from a set of toy figures,
brightly painted and brought to life,
each with a missing sliver
of humanity.

Their family stories change
with the shifting fogs,
but all are true and all false.

The Village's Fate

Some say the village will come to rest
at a place intended by whatever gods
from the beginning.
There, its constructed hill will set down
roots; there its pathways will unite
with the region's roads,
and the ephemeral villagers will
assimilate.

Others see the village picking up speed,
knocking other villages free
until the world is a carrom board
of terpen towns, sliding gracefully
together and again apart.

What few will admit is the fear
that neither is true, but that the fog
will one day swallow it, and all villages,
into oblivion.
Fewer still admit that this ending
is their hope.

About the Poet

Daniel Ausema's poetry and fiction have appeared in *Strange Horizons*, *Fantasy Magazine*, *Dreams & Nightmares*, and *Diabolical Plots*. His novels include the *Arcist Chronicles*, published by Guardbridge Books, and the steampunk-fantasy *Spire City* series. He is a member of the Science Fiction and Fantasy Poetry Association and has had works nominated for the Rhysling Award. He lives in Colorado, at the foot of the Rocky Mountains.

Publications by Island of Wak-Wak

Sublimation

Volume 1, Issue 1: Trauma (June 2024) — $11

Volume 1, Issue 2: Awe (July 2024) — $11

Volume 1, Issue 3: We Are Monsters All (August 2024) — $11

Volume 1, Issue 4: Every Party Needs a Bard (September/October 2024) — $11

Volume 1, Issue 5: Living in Another World (November/December 2024) — $11

Cabin Reading Series

Metamodern Morning Angst and Other Horrors by TS S. Fulk
ISBN: 978-9198959802 — $20 (Paperback)
ISBN: 979-8332306556 — $25 (Hardback)

The Ward at Twilight by Ken Anderson
ISBN: 978-9198959819 — $20 (Paperback)
ISBN: 978-9198959833 — $25 (Hardback)

Coffee Table Chapbook Series

Caffeinated by Annette Gagliardi
ISBN: 978-9198959826 — $12

Ephemeral Village by Daniel Ausema
ISBN: 978-9198959840 — $10

The Body Snatchers & Other Death Rituals by Kurt Newton
ISBN: 978-9198959857 — $12